Print information available on the last page

Rev. date: 02/16/2016

To order additional copies of this book,
contact:
Xlibris
1-888-795-4274
www.Xlibris.com
Orders@Xlibris.com

Who Is God?

By

Angel Abboud

Mommy who is God?
Adam asked.

Can I see Him?

Can He see me?

God is our father
God created you.
God created heaven
and earth and
everything you see.
Said Mommy.

God is in heaven.
God is a spirit and
He lives in our heart.
You cannot see Him.
But He can see you.

What is heaven?
Asked Adam

Heaven is the house
of God and the
angels.Heaven is
where we go when
we leave this world.
Heaven is a beautiful
and happy place.

God is someone
you pray to
everyday for what
you have. God is love
and peace.

God wants us to be good to one another and love each other all the time.

Whenever you had
a bad day pray to
God to make it
All better. He listens.

Don't forget to pray to God to thank Him for your blessings everyday.

Printed in the United States
By Bookmasters